ATLANTIS
SUBTERRANEAN TOURS

A Traveler's Guide
to the Lost City

Supervised and Edited by
Preston B. Whitmore

A Publication of
Whitmore Industries, Ltd.
Corporate and Dignitary Travel Division

a welcome book

EDITIONS
new york

Adapted from
Walt Disney Pictures Presents
Atlantis: The Lost Empire
Produced by Don Hahn
Directed by Gary Trousdale and Kirk Wise

Text by Jeff Kurtti

ISBN 07868-5328-X

Library of Congress Cataloging-in-Publication Data on file.

For information address
Disney Editions
114 Fifth Avenue
New York, New York 10011-5690

Disney Editions Editorial Director: Wendy Lefkon
Disney Editions Senior Editor: Sara Baysinger
Disney Editions Assistant Editor: Jody Revenson
Disney Editions Copy Chief: Monica Mayper
Disney Editions Senior Copy Editor: Christopher Caines

Produced by:
Welcome Enterprises, Inc.
588 Broadway
New York, New York 10011

Project Manager: Jacinta O'Halloran

Printed and bound in China by Toppan Printing Co., Inc.

First Edition

10 9 8 7 6 5 4 3 2 1

Visit www.disneyeditions.com

Contents

GREETINGS FROM PRESTON WHITMORE

This volume has been prepared for a specially selected assemblage of the most trustworthy and circumspect of my friends, associates, and colleagues. It is an essential guide and educational implement to amplify the enjoyment of your impending journey— and to enhance your appreciation of being one of a select few to be entrusted with the secrets of Atlantis.

Many celebrities, politicians, and world figures have made this exciting and unusual trip. Teddy Roosevelt, H.G. Wells, Harry Houdini, Jack London, and a group of descendants of Chief Seattle all have made the trip at my urging and invitation.

In freely sharing the dazzling and myriad secrets revealed by recent discoveries of the lost empire of Atlantis, it is understood that **each and every traveler must keep his or her experiences on this journey in the strictest confidence**. Acceptance of this book is a tacit and enforceable agreement of nondisclosure, and grants the traveler a Conditional Visa to enter the underground cavern that leads to Atlantis.

For visitors East of the Mississippi River:

Your journey will begin with your arrival at the Whitmore Enterprises Field Office in Cave City, Kentucky.

Your initial descent begins with a spelunking hike into Mammoth Cave, where a Whitmore Industries Guide will lead your party to the Atlantis approach fissure.

Your party is disguised as a common and unprepossessing Mammoth Caves tour group in order to preserve the anonymity of the Atlantis approach fissure.

Within the fissure there is a series of pathways that descends (with the assistance of a few strategically placed lifts and cog railways) to a section of the Atlantean Highway deep in the earth.

The occasional mechanized noise heard by the non-Atlantis-bound tourist is dismissed as a subterranean avalanche or one of the legendary "lost exploration parties" of Mammoth Caves (many of which well-known legends we have fabricated, as a cover story for our Atlantis activities within the Caves).

For visitors West of the Mississippi River:

Your journey will begin with your arrival at the Whitmore Enterprises Guano Harvesting Office in Carlsbad, New Mexico.

The initial descent to Atlantis begins with a car journey to the Carlsbad Caverns in New Mexico, where you will hike to an obscure cave called Slaughter Canyon Cave.

Here I have set up an elaborate system of elevators and cog railways that lowers travelers to a section of Atlantean Highway deep in the earth.

I have disguised this transport machinery by establishing a bat guano harvesting business in the mouth of the cave. The heavy machinery used in the guano harvesting masks the sound of the cog railway and acts as a decoy to uninvited guests.

Whitmore Industries actually makes a substantial profit from guano harvesting by shipping the product to California for use as fertilizer in the budding citrus industry!

The traveler must be aware of certain facts and restrictions in agreeing to the journey:

- Consider your physical limitations realistically when accepting a tour. Tours are not recommended for visitors who fear heights or close places and/or cannot climb steps. Do not let friends or family members talk you into joining a tour if you feel uncomfortable about it.

- Due to the self-contained environment, there are virtually no seasonal fluctuations in temperature. A year-round temperature of 72°F makes Atlantis a perfectly pleasant place. As we approach our destination, the temperature in the caverns hovers around 54°F year-round, so a light jacket is recommended for this portion of the journey.

- Hard-packed dirt trails can be somewhat rough and uneven and may be wet and slippery. You'll encounter numerous stairs and steep inclines on many cave tours. Therefore, durable, flat-soled footwear suitable for walking is essential.

- Walking sticks and canes are permitted on tours only when sufficient need is demonstrated.

- Smoking is not permitted en route.

- Photography is prohibited.

- For reasons of secrecy and security, all visitors will be blindfolded after a determined point within the Atlantean Road Approach Caverns, and will remain so until the destination is reached.

These few restrictions are trifling compared to the wonders that await you upon arrival. I look forward to seeing you in Atlantis!

Your Obedient Servant,

Preston B. Whitmore

Preston B. Whitmore

Atlantis in Brief

Being Essential Information in Digest Form for the Traveler

BEFORE YOU TRAVEL: PASSPORTS AND VISAS

United States Citizens

All U.S. citizens, even infants, need only a valid passport to enter Atlantis for stays of up to 30 days. Application forms for first-time and renewal passports are available in U.S. Passport Agency offices and at most large municipal post offices and/or court-houses. Passports are valid for ten years and are usually mailed within four to six weeks.

Canadian Citizens

Canadian citizens need only a valid passport to enter Atlantis for stays of up to 30 days. Passport application forms are available in regional passport offices and at most large municipal post offices as well as travel agencies. You must apply in person. Children under 16 years of age may travel on their parents' passport but must have their own to travel alone. Passports are valid for five years and are usually mailed within two to three weeks.

Citizens of the United Kingdom

Citizens of the U.K. need only a valid passport to enter Atlantis for stays of up to 30 days. Application forms for first-time and renewal passports are available in most large municipal post offices and in passport offices. You must apply in person. Children under 16 years of age may travel on their parents' passport but must have their own to travel alone. All passports are valid for ten years, and are usually mailed within four weeks.

YOUR ARRIVAL IN ATLANTIS: WHAT TO EXPECT

The trip on the Atlantean highway will require travelers to use oxygen tanks and frequently "pop their ears," to relieve the internal pressure. Once at the Atlantean Highway, you will get your first taste of the inner world when you are met by an Atlantean greeting party, who will feed you, entertain you, and put you to sleep for the night (to have time to acclimate to the underground environment).

In the "morning," (morning is when the lava fields in this section of the caves rise in level and create a source of light), a series of vehicles then form a convoy to Atlantis. Along the way, you will be

ATLANTIS IN BRIEF

OVERVIEW

DINING

LODGING

NIGHTLIFE & ARTS

SHOPPING

TOURS

PHRASES

treated to Atlantean music and folklore, and an introduction to the indigenous creatures in the caves in and around Atlantis.

Visitors enjoy their first views of Atlantis from the same vantage point that Milo Thatch and the original Whitmore Expedition enjoyed. The convoy pauses for a moment at the edge of the Atlantean grotto to take in the view before proceeding across the Entrance Bridge into the old city.

There is a brief ceremony (the equivalent to a customs procedure) where visitors will once again be reminded of the confidentiality that they must keep. Then, the travelers are escorted with their baggage to their first night's lodging.

Emergencies *Police*

Peace officers are located throughout city. Look for pictograms and directional signage on every street.

Medical emergencies

Emergency medical service is available 24 hours every day at the Foreigners' Department of Kashekem Nedakh Memorial Hospital (Circle Dihn North). Also, medical service is available weekdays, 8:00 AM until 8:00 PM, at the First Medical Clinic of Atlantis (Circle Say East).

Dentists

Circle Dihn North, adjacent to Nedakh Memorial, emergency dental service is available 24 hours every day.

Late night pharmacies

There are two 24-hour pharmacies close to the interior ring of the city, specializing in crystal healing and the abundantly available herbal ton-ics, poultices, and remedies that are a specialty of Atlantean medicine. (Look for pictogram adja-cent to Nedakh Memorial, also in the Wehsertem of the Atlantean Grand Hotel.)

Visitor Information Nehsettem Wehgehnohsuhg (Traveler's Office) is located in the city center, immediately south of the Central Wehsertem, with branch offices located in each city circle, east and west. The first stop for general tourist information, the Nehsettem has updates on events, festivals, public performances, as well as detailed city maps. They can also exchange money, arrange tickets or tours, and help with special needs.

Language The Atlantean language is based on a root dialect, akin to the Tower of Babel. The great explorer and linguist Milo Thatch theorized that deconstructed Latin, overlaid with Sumerian, and a dash of Thessalian, was their basic grammatical structure, which is almost exactly like certain obscure offshoots of Choctaw (using Creek pronunciation). Thatch believed this proof positive that Atlantean trade routes accessed the New World centuries before the Bronze Age.

Most Atlanteans are quite frankly amazing in their linguistic prowess. Visitors can expect to hear Latin, Italian, Hebrew, French, German, Greek, even Chinese. If the idea of attempting to speak the Atlantean mother tongue is daunting, you will easily find a conversational language that is comfortable.

Health There are few serious health hazards for the traveler in Atlantis. It is recommended that the visitor slowly escalate in their intake of Atlantean epicurean delicacies, as too many such treats too quickly may bring a shock to the system. The running water may taste strange to the visitor, many being used to the lamentable state of most urban water supplies.

To avoid problems clearing customs, diabetic travelers carrying needles and syringes should have on hand a letter from their physician confirming their need for insulin injections.

Mail No transfer of written communication is allowed from Atlantis to the Outer World. Important communications and messages for family and friends may be transmitted through your Whitmore Industries representative. Mail within the city is picked up at the marked kiosk on an average of three times daily, depending on the demand.

Telephones Atlanteans place a high value on face-to-face communication. Therefore, Atlantis has no telephone system. This makes intercity communication challenging for the Outer World visitor, but any hotel concierge, hospitality staff, or tourist office will be glad to assist visitors in contacting any person or business within the city.

Whitmore Industries and former explorer Mrs. Wilhelmina Packard have arranged for phone communications to the Outer World. The system is a form of wireless communication that relies on the conductive properties of igneous rock with high metal content. The system is crude, but allows callers to talk for up to 30 seconds to people on the surface, and is very useful in case of emergency. For security reasons, the staff at Whitmore Industries monitors all calls.

Money The unit of currency in Atlantis is the kurhauna ("king" or "crown," abbreviated *Kû*) which is divided into ten dehkep. There are coins of 1, 2, and 5 dehkep; coins of 1, 2, 5, 10, 20, and 50 *Kû*; and notes *Kû* of 20, 50, 100, 200, 500, 1,000, and 5,000 *Kû*. As everywhere in the Outer World, exact change is always appreciated.

The best place to exchange Outer World money for Atlantean is at the main Nehsettem Wehgehnohsuhg in the city center, immediately south of the Central Wehsertem, or one of the branch offices located in each city circle, east and west. At the time of publication, one *Kû* trades for about US$1.13.

What It Costs

Cup of coffee: *Kû* 1.25	One mile in hired vehicle: *Kû* 1.90
Theater seat: *Kû* 35-100	Museum admission: *Kû* 5.00
Pint of ale: *Kû* 1.25	Glass of Atlantean wine: *Kû* 5
	Bottle of Atlantean wine: *Kû* 40-150

Kû

Try to avoid changing money at hotels or other business, as our Outer World currency is essentially valueless to them, which means they must make an extra effort to secure exchange with the Whitmore Industries representatives.

Tipping To reward good service in a restaurant, round the bill up to the nearest multiple of ten (if the bill comes to 53 *Kû*, for example, give the waiter 60 *Kû*); 10% is considered appropriate on very large tabs. Tip the bell person who brings bags to your room 2 to 5 *Kû*. For Room Service, 2 *Kû* is plenty. In hired vehicles, round the fare up by 10%. Give tour docents, hospitality staff, and concierges between 5 and 10 *Kû* depending upon services rendered.

Transportation within Atlantis Atlantis is a pedestrian-friendly environment laid out in an ingenious pattern of concentric circles crosscut with canals. Pedestrian transport is fairly easy throughout the city, but pictograms along each circle and canal will alert the visitor to available boat transportation. In addition, Atlantean hover-vehicles are available for hire, and are enjoyed as much for their peculiarity as for their efficiency. Hover vehicles may be hailed from the ground or can usually be found standing at marked locations throughout the city. Rates are on an hourly basis.

Tour Operators Whitmore Industries operates the only tours of Atlantis authorized for visitors from the Outer World. *Within* Atlantis, day excursions can be easily arranged through the Whitmore representative, hotel concierge or hospitality staff, or by contacting the tourist office.

Guided Tours Nehsettem Wehgehnohsuhg (Traveler's Office, above) sponsors several tours of the city for residents and visitors from the Outer World. A three-hour "Historical Atlantis" tour is offered year-round, and combines walking, watercraft, and hover-vehicle views of the majestic city, guided by an informed and informative Atlantean docent. Schedule varies according to demand. Also check for the availability of the "Architectural Atlantis" and "Artisans of Atlantis" tours, which feature smaller groups and more personal interaction with the locales and citizenry.

Opening and Closing Times

Atlanteans are both notoriously blasé and famously accommodating regarding hours of business. Shopkeepers and service people will arrive when the city begins to stir and close when it seems appropriate. They will often leave their places of business during what Outer Worlders consider "business hours," but are more than happy to make appointments, which they keep precisely and consider a point of honor.

Customs and Duties

To speed your clearance through customs, keep receipts for all of your purchases in Atlantis and be ready to show the purchases to the inspector. If you feel you have been incorrectly or unfairly charged a duty, ask to see a supervisor. You are entitled to appeal any assessments in dispute.

National Holidays

January 1: All Kings' Day (Celebration of the Crystal)
April: Festival of Arts
June: Summer Harvest
September: Celebration of Sports and Gaming
December: Winter Harvest

Monthly dances are a much-anticipated social event (check with Nehsettem Wehgehnohsuhg for schedule).

ATLANTIS IN BRIEF

OVERVIEW

DINING

LODGING

NIGHTLIFE & ARTS

SHOPPING

TOURS

PHRASES

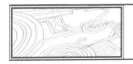 
NONDISCLOSURE AGREEMENT

Agreement, entered into as of _____ , _____ between
_____ (hereinafter referred to
as "The Traveler"), and Whitmore Industries, Ltd.

In consideration of the opportunity to visit Atlantis,
The Traveler agrees not to discuss or divulge any
portion of said place or contents thereof to any third
party, other than employees of Whitmore Industries,
Ltd. and its representatives. The Traveler agrees to
return the <u>Traveler's Guide to The Lost City</u> to a
Whitmore Industries representative upon completion of
their stay in Atlantis and not to discuss or disclose
any portion of said guide to any third party, other
than employees of Whitmore Industries, Ltd. and its
representatives. In the event such an agreement is
made, the parties will include appropriate provisions
for all steps reasonably necessary and proper to preserve the confidentiality of the journey, location, and
secrets of Atlantis. If no such agreement is made, it
is understood and agreed that breach of confidentiality
by either of the undersigned will cause serious and
irreparable harm for which the aggrieved party may seek
the appropriate remedy. This agreement shall terminate
in the event the location or contents thereof become
public knowledge through no fault of Whitmore
Industries, Ltd.

This agreement must be executed in person.

Whitmore Industries, Ltd.

_____   _____
Preston B. Whitmore   Traveler

An Overview of Atlantis
Being a Brief Familiarization with the History and Culture of Atlantis

A SHORT HISTORY OF ATLANTIS

The story of Atlantis was first recorded in the Outer World by the Greek philosopher Plato (c. 427 B.C. - 347 B.C.) in 360 B.C., in his dialogues *Timaeus* and *Critias*. Although Plato used Atlantis as an allegory, to teach the perils of greed, insolence, and brutality and demonstrate the punishment meted out by heaven to those who worship false gods, he also asserted that the foundational story was *true*.

Atlantis in ancient times was a continent of the Atlantic Ocean, a land of plentitude; a true earthly paradise where want was unknown and peace was a way of life. The island itself was a great lush plain surrounded on three sides by immense embracing mountains. The excellent soil was source to all manner of trees and plants, and the continent bloomed with plentiful flora, all of which contributed to a rich agrarian industry. Wealthy villages and hamlets could be found in the hills and mountains, and their meadows, woods, and fields were home to an amazing variety of indigenous animals.

A Mighty Power Source It is said that tens of thousands of years ago, a giant comet passed close to the earth, and 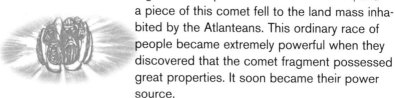 a piece of this comet fell to the land mass inhabited by the Atlanteans. This ordinary race of people became extremely powerful when they discovered that the comet fragment possessed great properties. It soon became their power source.

To a large degree, it even became a deity: The main crystal was like a power plant, a giant amorphous ball of light that floated high above the city, giving its light and life to all. In turn, each Atlantean wore a small shard of the mother crystal around his or her neck. This personal crystal was used to heal and was found to bring unusually long life. It was constantly recharged by the mother crystal, or as the Atlanteans called it, "The Heart of Atlantis."

A Fall from Grace Over time, it is said, the Atlanteans utilized their technological power to dominate other civilizations. They used the crystal to fuel a powerful armada and waged war with incredible strength, but their hubris caused a great accident, and the power of the crystals wiped the Atlanteans off the face of the earth.

After the Fall The aforementioned Milo Thatch found in his study of Atlantis that the benevolent crystals saved Atlantis with a massive force field, but the holocaust drove Atlantis deep into the center of the earth and caused a great flood to sweep over the planet. (The flood was memorialized in the biblical book of Genesis.)

The ancient leaders of Atlantis, and in particular its king, Kashekem Nedakh, vowed to keep the power of the crystals a secret forever to prevent a reoccurrence of this traumatic time. The king ordered all accounts of history to be destroyed and he hid the crystal deep beneath the city of Atlantis where it was meant to stay forever like a genie in a bottle. In time, the Atlanteans became a peaceful tribal culture whose people lived along the water's edge in their lost underground city. Atlantis was a romantic ruin whose population lost track of their once-great history.

The Shepherd's It was my great fortune many years ago in
Journal my youth to make the acquaintance of one Thaddeus T. Thatch. While I had an interest in the study of commerce, Thatch was always fascinated with the fringes of archaeology. We studied at Georgetown and became closest friends. I would bore him with stories of railroad fortunes, factories, and industrial development, and he would retort with theories of lost civilizations: the Anasazi, Lemuria, Mu, and, of course, his obsession, Atlantis.

ATLANTIS IN BRIEF

OVERVIEW

DINING

LODGING

NIGHTLIFE & ARTS

SHOPPING

TOURS

PHRASES

Thatch spent much of his life in pursuit of something called *The Scrolls of Aziz*, or more commonly, *The Shepherd's Journal*. This fascinating relic was said to be a firsthand account of Atlantis and its exact whereabouts.

One day a shepherd named Aziz was tending his flock near a mountainous region of what is now Syria, when he slipped into a rift in the ground and disappeared. He returned a full *two years* later, babbling about an amazing place that he had found. He was branded a lunatic and thrown into an asylum, where he wrote a detailed account of his journey in a strange language that the people of his day thought was simply the mad nonsense and gibberish of a deluded crank. The scrolls came to be known in modern times as *The Shepherd's Journal*, and have been acknowledged by scholars to be an encrypted but detailed account of a journey to the ancient continent of Atlantis—actually written in the Atlantean language.

The Whitmore Expedition In the early part of this century, I funded an expedition to Iceland to find the journal. When Thatch actually did find the darn thing (much to my chagrin), he brought it to Washington, D.C., for study, and here, Thatch planned on translating the Journal and publishing his findings in the *National Review of Archaeology and Science*, an important academic periodical.

I was prepared to take the translated journal and mount an expedition to Atlantis, to honor Thatch and prove his genius to the world. Sadly, Thatch died on the return trip to Washington, leaving the cryptic journal in my possession, addressed to his grandson, Milo James Thatch. He said if anything were to happen to him, I should give it to Milo.

Now, even though Thaddeus Thatch was gone, God rest his soul, Preston Whitmore is a man who keeps his word. If I could bring back just *one* shred of proof that his theories were valid,

that would be satisfactory for me. I knew that Milo Thatch was the key to such an expedition. (Thatch and a couple of million dollars' worth of hardware, anyway.)

Milo jumped at the chance to partake in an expedition to Atlantis, and as far as the rest of the expedition crew, I got the best of the best. They're the same crew that brought the Journal back. That expedition went on one of the almightiest adventures I've ever heard of, and is the reason you're holding this book today in preparation for one of the almightiest adventures you'll ever have.

For some time, I have purposely obfuscated the facts of the mission for a number of reasons. A discovery of such magnitude, a power source of such enormity, and the damage the secrets of Atlantis could do to the world (let alone the danger it might cause those who were the custodians of those secrets)....Well, the whole darn thing was just too dangerous to reveal to the world...especially the way that world was looking in those darkening days toward the end of 1914.

But now, for a specially selected assemblage of

Protection from Without:
The Fearsome Leviathan

For ages, a fearsome airborne and submersible unmanned attack vehicle known as the Leviathan has protected Atlantis. It draws its energy, as all Atlantean vehicles do, from the mother crystal that sustains Atlantis. (How that power is channeled for motion or weaponry is unknown.) The Leviathan is somewhat lobster-shaped, making it very maneuverable and agile—both in the air and underwater. Its energy beam weapon is tremendously powerful.

There is speculation that it is this defensive vehicle that is described in the book of Job (41:1). The Bible says, "Out of his mouth go burning lights, sparks of fire shoot out."

the most trustworthy and circumspect of my friends, associates, and colleagues; I am pleased to bid you *Weeltem Ahdluhntihsuhg net Gahwindihn Nahgebyoakh* — a joyous welcome to Atlantis!

– P.B.W.

ATLANTIS TODAY

The core of Atlantis today is its great capital (also called Atlantis), a city comprised of once-grand buildings made of red, black, and white stone. Atlantis sits atop a tabletop formation and is completely surrounded with waterfalls. The city's enveloping cavern was carved out eons ago, when Atlantis first submerged to this location from the surface of the Outer World. When Atlantis sank, it was surrounded by a force field that melted, vaporized, and reshaped the surrounding bedrock. When the molten rock cooled and the force field was inactivated, the cavern that now encloses Atlantis was created.

Over the ages, the forces of nature and gravity have shaped, softened, and shifted the cavern, so it has a mysterious, almost eerie otherworldly appearance. Organic shapes merge and blend with architectural ones, and the population lives in a thriving new society within and alongside the ruins of its former culture.

The Capital The capital is laid out in concentric circles. The entire outer wall is coated with brass, and a second, interior wall is sheathed with tin, and a third wall, the one which encloses the palace, flashes with the red light of an element known only in Atlantis and called *oricalcum*.

Today, the upper reaches of Atlantis are mostly deserted and empty, the only real inhabitant of the upper city since the Cataclysm was King Kashekim Nedakh. While still beautiful and fascinating, this region is somewhat quiet and ghostly.

Population The thriving population has migrated to the colorful and lively waterfront, and the market area there has the tumult and vibrancy of a little Hong Kong. During ancient times, the waterfront was home to a bustling seaport, with merchants,

ATLANTIS IN BRIEF · OVERVIEW · DINING · LODGING · NIGHTLIFE & ARTS · SHOPPING · TOURS · PHRASES

traders, and sailors arriving from and departing for ports of call all over the ancient world. Today, the waterfront maintains the energy, if not the function of its ancient past.

The population is here out of necessity, since they depend on hydro-farming, fishing (net-casting from boats or spear fishing along the shorelines), trapping (sea creatures, etc.), and some livestock ranching (ostrich-like birds, giant slugs, giant crabs). This congregation of activities has led to the establishment of the lively Waterfront Wehsertem, a marketplace/bazaar that any visitor *must* see and experience.

Getting Around Atlantis To see Atlantis and all its wonders, there is no better alternative to walking. There are roads and walkways throughout the city, but most of the vehicles are of the flying or hovering variety. There are a number of large paved areas that aren't connected to anything other than by walkways or stairways—these are landing parks for the Atlantean vehicles. With the city's abundant waterways and canals, small watercraft (much like the gondolas of Venice) are all around, as are more substantial barges and boats for river and port commerce.

Although it is no longer in service, there is also an elevated monorail system that once traversed the city. Although inoperable, this monorail is still well worth looking at, since its cars are meticulously carved and look like stylized dragon fish. Some of Atlantis's concentric rings are canals and aqueducts, some are the ruined tracks for this monorail.

Air, Light, Water, and Power The great power source of the Atlantean crystals creates the warm Atlantean "daylight" which is cycled into a day-night pattern similar to the Outer World. Science has yet to determine exactly *how* this crystalline "battery" actually *works*. The crystals also act as a kind of massive recirculating pump system, perpetually refreshing the water and air supplies of the city.

ATLANTIS IN BRIEF

OVERVIEW

DINING

LODGING

NIGHTLIFE & ARTS

SHOPPING

TOURS

PHRASES

The Heart of Atlantis draws water from the ocean miles above through honeycomb fissures down into Atlantis itself, where the water is purified and falls into the tabletop "flat earth" sea, via the scores of picturesque waterfalls around the city. The water in the surrounding "sea" overflows the rim and cascades over the side and onto a constantly flowing river of molten lava. The lava has been flowing here from the time of the Cataclysm, and is kept in check by the constant pounding of the waterfalls.

Climate The resulting steam is what makes the Atlantean climate much like that of a tropical island: warm and on the muggy side. Rain is frequent, but as in the tropics of the Outer World, no one pays much attention. This climate accounts for the abundant vegetation of Atlantis. The high humidity caused by the constant interaction of water and lava creates a giant hothouse for a boggling variety of verdant tropical plants that grow from the cavern walls and on the buildings of Atlantis itself.

The Atlanteans For long ages, the Atlantean people appreciated their blessings of abundance and lived self-supported, and at peace with the rest of the world. They were untainted by their possessions and great wealth, and spent their lives engaged in activities of generosity and gentility. Their primary avocations were education, cultivating virtue, living in peace with each other and in harmony with nature.

The citizens of Atlantis are warm, friendly, and accommodating, if a touch on the primitive side. This is reasonable, since as their empire collapsed, their culture slowly declined from predominantly high-tech/agriculture to that of hunter-fisher-gatherers.

The Atlanteans still lead a very civic life, however. Among the many still-used buildings of ancient Atlantis are numerous temples, and there are verdant public and private gardens all about. Gathering places such as markets, baths, gymnasiums, racecourses, even a horse racing track are all a vibrant part of the public fabric of Atlantis.

In recent years, through the efforts of Queen Kida and Milo Thatch, the Atlantean culture has been on the ascent, the citizens relearning many of their old customs, languages, and technologies. Atlantis is again very much a civilization on the rise.

The Atlanteans' physical appearance is distinctive and unusual. Their comportment has a kinetic serenity that is almost hypnotic to Outer Worlders, with the result that most foreigners find the Atlanteans quite soothingly beautiful without being able to explain exactly why.

Native Dress The Atlanteans tend to dress in loose-fitting and somewhat short or abbreviated attire, due to the heat and humidity; and their textiles are often brightly colored and usually exquisitely wrought. Hunters and guardsmen or other law enforcement officers, use a kind of primitive body armor fashioned from scales and/or body plates from some of the more ferocious cave-dwelling animals.

The Heart of Atlantis and Personal Power The citizens of Atlantis tend to live a very long time, and age rather slowly as a result of the effects of the Heart of Atlantis crystal and the smaller crystals that each Atlantean carries. These smaller crystals, which most people wear around their necks, are like personal "batteries."

A NOTE ABOUT LANGUAGE: The Atlantis visitor might find it bizarre to see an abundance of Atlantean language, place names, and signage only to be confronted with a restaurant with an Italian name or a shop bearing a Chinese one. Atlantis was for many ages a seaport city, the crossroads of the world. Over the eons, dozens of different external influences have found their way into the Atlantean culture, so don't be surprised to see an occasional "foreigner" who has set up shop here.

They hold a "charge" for a while, but they require the greater power of the Heart of Atlantis to sustain their force of energy.

The vehicles and smaller machinery have small shards of crystal imbedded inside that either work in conjunction with the personal crystals that the Atlanteans carry, or with the main city grid.

Native Dwellings The average Atlanteans live mostly in hollowed-out giant gourds that grow from the waterside trees. The carving work on these habitats is quite intricate and the long Atlantean life spans have provided many years for their design and execution.

Most of the Atlanteans live and work along the waterfronts, as that is where the predominant survival livelihoods exist: the hydro farming, fishing, and trapping mentioned earlier. There are other populations and living spaces, however, related to other pursuits, tasks, and crafts; including weaving, basketry, pottery, wood and stone carving, metalworking and smelting, and textile and clothing manufacture.

In addition, a portion of the population is employed as agrarian gatherers, collecting plants, roots, and flora, along with necessary woods (including firewood).

A Benevolent Monarchy The government of Atlantis has for eons been a benevolent monarchy, and remains so to this day. After the Cataclysm, King Kashekim Nedakh felt an enormous personal responsibility for the destruction of his former empire and of the ancient paradise over which he ruled, but behind his tortured disposition lay a wise leader and loving father. The secret he kept was his only assurance that the past would not repeat itself, even though the cost was the gradual extinction of his people. His final years were haunted with the burden of his responsibility, and he maintained a self-imposed exile in the

ATLANTIS IN BRIEF

OVERVIEW

DINING

LODGING

NIGHTLIFE & ARTS

SHOPPING

TOURS

PHRASES

decaying palace, and seldom addressed his people.

Kida After the passing of King Kashekim Nedakh, the new queen, Kida, discovered the secrets of her past and the events that led to the demise of her nation. As she ascended the throne, her willful, resourceful, and trusting nature served her well; but by mixing among the people, she lived in distinct contrast to her father's reclusive temperament. Together with Milo Thatch, an explorer from the Outer World, her strong leadership and altruism have been the key to a cultural renaissance in Atlantis.

It is because of this resurrection that you have the remarkable opportunity to visit the lost empire of Atlantis, and to partake of the utterly unique sights and sounds of this fantastic realm.

Dining
Being an Epicurean Advisor to the Atlantis Visitant

By necessity, the Atlantean diet tends to be seafood-based. Overall, it is on the spicy side, sharing preparation and ingredient traits of Indian and Thai food. Atlanteans eat four small meals each day (breakfast, brunch, lunch, and dinner), along with a large early-evening feast that is a daily culinary and social event.

Beware, though, many of the utensils are bewildering and difficult to the Outer Worlders. There are strange thumb-and-finger cups, connected with a wire about six inches long. Food is snared and swung into the mouth with this one. Then there's an egg-whisk/spatula/spiral object that is used as a kind of spoon. It takes a good deal of practice to eat with either of these.

Note that soup is drunk directly from the bowls, and eating it in other fashion is considered vulgar, or even comical.

A popular portable food is squid tentacle on a stick. Boiled in a choice of a spicy or sweet broth, and served up wrapped on a skewer-stick, the consumer sucks it down like a giant spaghetti.

For a quick alternative to the mainly sit-down establishments listed below, you may wish to try a light meal at one of the city's growing number of street stands or food carts.

HOME DINING

Often, the natives will simply invite strangers in to dine in their homes, a long-standing Atlantean custom. Though Outer Worlders might find it disquieting at first, it is an unparalleled way to gain a true understanding of Atlantis and her people.

Atlanteans display symbols of welcome and entrée on their homes at mealtimes. Visitors should feel no fear about approaching these homes and seeking a place at the table. Seldom will an Atlantean refuse a request for a meal from a visiting stranger, and the Atlanteans are as curious about the Outer World as visitors are about the natives. Often meals are taken outside of the dwelling, and passing strangers will simply be invited to step in.

A contribution to the meal is usually accepted in lieu of any real "payment," and the typical Atlantean regards a generous compliment or a sincere appreciation of equal value with currency. Carry a bottle of good Atlantean wine when you are seeking a home meal, or a dessert or side dish, or ingredients for a future meal. A cash gift is also acceptable, but lacks the grace of these alternate methods of consideration.

Below are brief listings of some of the more generous and renowned homes:

Mother Kurth Ehvish If you wonder what it might feel like to have grown up in Atlantis and go back to Mom's house for a Sunday dinner, this is the house to stop in. There is nothing ostentatious or offbeat here. The surroundings are warm, comfortable, and well-used; the meals are simple, satisfying, and nutritious. Naturally, Mother's desserts are similarly simple and sweet, as is the hostess. Mother often stubbornly refuses even the most miniscule gratuity, whether edible or monetary, and "squabbling" with mother over payment has actually become a beloved custom of the house. *22 Shoreline Drive*

Shadehm House Shadehm is something of an Atlantean character, a sort of grand, eccentric, and charming "Auntie Mame." A visit to her house is always lively and always entertaining. The meals usually consist of a series of excellent (and filling) appetizers created from a variety of fresh local fruits, vegetables, baked goods, and seafoods. Shadehm is always on the move, circulating among her guests. The house is decorated with memorabilia and mementos of Shadehm's great career as a singer and entertainer. *23 Beekman Place*

Wóhl Skhee The home of one of the most prominent and beloved artists in Atlantis, Wóhl Skhee, this house is also one of the friendliest. Laughter is abundant here, and fits well with warmth and the good taste of the home's decor. You may come at mealtime, but don't be surprised to find yourself lingering long after your repast is done, discussing everything from the New

Hebrides to igneous rock formations with your gregarious host. The works of the artist are displayed throughout the dwelling. Wóhl Skhee was a Barrista in his youth, and serves an unparalleled Atlantean cappuccino.

72 Marietta Street

Dahnhahn House The genial bearded patriarch of this particular house not only encourages visitors, but also enjoys getting a group of people into the kitchen to help him prepare the meals. Dahnhahn has a way of assembling a dinner party so that the guests tend to fascinate each other, and his involving methods of preparing a meal guarantee that everyone feels that they have truly had a part in the repast that they share and enjoy. The host is renowned for an Atlantean comfort food similar to the American corn dog.

24 Riverside Drive

Guide to Ratings

$$$$	More than 40	$$	15-25
$$$	25-40	$	Less than 15

Per person for a typical three-course meal, excluding wine and tip.

RESTAURANTS

Most restaurants are open-air, with many located along the docks and waterfront or in thatch-roofed structures built on pilings *in* the water. The atmosphere is informal and convivial; the visitor is encouraged to make himself comfortable and to yield to the renowned Atlantean hospitality.

Wehgehnohsuhg The menu of Wehgehnohsuhg will feel familiar **(The Traveler)** to Outer Worlders—they feature 20 pasta dishes and nine pizzas, along with fish courses. Another specialty of the house is a variety of flavorful omelets. Perched on its stiltlike pilings, Wehgehnohsuhg offers a wonderful view of the water as well as the hurly-burly of the waterfront district and its Wehsertem. As far as the sights, there isn't a bad seat in the house, and it is easy to assemble any kind of meal from a late snack to a full evening feast from components of the Wehgehnohsuhg menu. Their traditional Atlantean desserts are an unexpected pleasure, and they have a good selection of wines for such an informal surrounding. **$**

91 Shoreline Gangway

Nahwehnohsuhg (The Swimmer) The Swimmer derives its name from the fact that, unlike its neighbors on stilts, Nahwehnohsuhg rides low in the water, taking advantage of the unique views from the waterline. Visually, its design is less concerned with its outside views than with its central cooking pit, which is actually a lava fissure. Foods are grilled, seared, and smoked over the circulating lava. Fish entrees are the most popular here, but the steaks and smoked meats are outstanding, as is the grilled vegetable selection. Desserts are light and fruit-based. The service is a little slow, but worth the wait, since the proprietors have compensated with a fine list of Atlantean ales for sampling. The outside deck is a comfortable lounging area if that activity will be your primary one. **$$$**

41 Shoreline (Take the right gangway — avoid the rope bridge!)

Nahr Bahdehgbay ("Best Place") The loose translation is less clumsy than the actual Atlantean, which means literally "a place where you may enjoy comfort with quality." Heavy furnishings reportedly rescued from an ancient family home "up the hill" add an oddly formal touch to an otherwise relaxed surrounding, and the menu features a huge selection of traditional Atlantean dishes, with an emphasis on meat and seafood. Especially worthwhile are the cornbread with Atlantean goat cheese, cheese pie, and meat-filled pastry. Often a live performance is part of the meal service, and frequently the featured performer remains to visit with the assembled guests. **$$**

Nahr Bahdehgbay can be reached by the launch from Beach-head Cusp. Look for the "Narwhal."

ATLANTIS IN BRIEF

OVERVIEW

DINING

LODGING

NIGHTLIFE & ARTS

SHOPPING

TOURS

PHRASES

The Captain's Table

A tribute to the importance of the sea for Atlantis both past and present, The Captain's Table offers the finest seafood meals available not only in Atlantis, but anywhere in the known world. The restaurant building has actually been fashioned into the interior of a grand sailing ship that was beached during the Cataclysm, and its nautical decor is both opulent and authentic. The two-pepper soup is a specialty, as are the seafood chowders that change daily. Your server will provide you with at least half a dozen daily fresh catch specials. For a seafood lover, the sheer number of choices may prove frustrating. Window seats afford breathtaking waterfall views. **$$$**
51 Beach-head Crest

The Garden Court

Although travelers may feel that hotel restaurants lack the panache of other dining spots, The Garden Court at the Atlantean Grand Hotel is an exception. Realizing that they face a great deal of competition from the more lively waterfront establishments, the management here has both focused on the needs and desires of its tenant clientele and created some terrific enticements to get the locals to come "up the hill." Among the latter are a weekly wine tasting and exceptional live entertainment. The surroundings are pure Atlantis, pre-Cataclysm. The finest of the hand arts that the ancients could create abound within the walls of the garden court, and the garden isn't just a name: the atrium overflows with a bounty of native Atlantean flora. This is just the place for a quiet, romantic meal for two, or a splendid retreat when you've had enough of the waterfront's energy. **$$$**
12 Circle Dihn North

HIGH-END DINING

High-end dining is mostly the domain of the floating restaurant barges. The dinner barges are either moored right next to one another or connected via gangways or a series of smaller boats tied in between. It is entirely possible to wander around for hours, and on dozens of boats, while remaining entirely "on foot."

Ahdluhntihsuhg
(The Atlantis)

This majestic-looking waterfront institution is truly represented by its name; both in decor and menu, it is almost a history of Atlantis itself. The building and interiors that seem to totter precariously over the falls, have been assembled from salvaged ruins of the ancient pre-Cataclysm Atlantis and appended with carvings, crafts, and architectural modifications from after the fall. The menu is a sampling of Atlantean cuisine from the Empire to the present, and many meals from around the world (who knows *how* they got a recipe for Beef Wellington, but here it is). Although an evening spent at Ahdluhntihsuhg can be quite pricey, there is really nothing like it anywhere in the world, and it is almost a primer for the entire Atlantis experience. **$$$$**
Number 24 Dockside

Kan-Lis

Founded by Kan-Lis and currently run by his son and daughter-in-law, this is *the* dining institution of Atlantis. When an Atlantean citizen wants an elegant night on the town, this is typically the place they will choose. Located in the finest floating barge at the city's best moorage, the Kan-Lis is the site of generations of engagement dinners, wedding anniversary parties, birthday celebrations, and prom dates. The menu is sometimes criticized for being conservative, but an institution is seldom a culinary laboratory. The chef has made sure that everything on the menu is the finest that can be accomplished, and disappointment is never a side dish here. The desserts are a must, and the live orchestra and dancing are a lovely and elegant touch. **$$$$**
Number 76 Aurora Moorage

Alphonse's The habitués of this Atlantean institution know the place — they call it Alpho's — the menu, and each other very well. For decades, many of the finest senior artists and craftsmen of Atlantis have made this their haunt, especially during the lunch and dinner times. The menu is varied, if somewhat unimaginative, and tending toward the Atlantean versions of "steaks and chops." The rose of smoked salmon with dill mayonnaise is a terrific starter, and the grilled trout is delicious. The interior is a masculine warm and woody decor with the feeling of an old men's club, and the bar can be quite lively, as it is popular with the barge-hopping crowd. **$$$$**
Number 79 Riverside Moorage

PUBS AND SMOKE HOUSES

Drinking establishments tend toward small neighborhood-based pubs with regular — and often colorful — local clientele. Smoke Houses are akin to Outer World cigar lounges, or like "lodges," where natives gather to relax, socialize, and discuss current events and issues.

Kohnoshuhg Teekudehtoat (Train Station) This cozy (if somewhat noisy) pub takes its name from its location under the central platform of the (now defunct) municipal monorail system. The dimly lit interior is a veritable museum of Atlantean public transit, with signage, art, posters, schedules, and paper collateral material tracing the entire history of the monorail and other modes of transport. The ale and wine lists are simple and straightforward, and the food offerings are spare and tend toward the fried, which is probably just as well. This is an honest pub where the honest working stiffs of Atlantis feel most at home. **$**
34 Circle Doot North

PagoPago This is the king of all "artist's" pubs, a gathering place for the artisans and craftsmen of Atlantis for generations. Don't look for finery or fancy decor: the byword of the PagoPago is functionality. The character of the place derives not from its setting, but from its characters: its habitués tend to be the brightest and most fascinating of Atlantis's creative citizenry. The floor show here is the discussion, debate, demonstration, and dart games among the several generations of artists who populate this place, (in various states of inebriation), from the early hours of the morning to the wee hours of the night. The food service is sparse, but there is a chili-like concoction that can't be touched in the Outer World, served with fresh-baked corn bread, and a garlic soup that is properly legendary. **$**
45 Alahmeeduh Avenue

Ohbehsuhg Kehloabtem (Lava Room) Located in a basement, the Lava Room is the Atlantean equivalent of a small Manhattan lounge (or the bar of the most commercial hotel in any city hosting a World's Fair). A little cool, a little…well…sleazy, the Ohbehsuhg caters to the "Martini Trade" of Atlantis. The young business people flock here for the somewhat rare Atlantean mixed cocktails and the entertainment, which tends toward keyboard and vocalists crooning Atlantean pop standards. This is the kind of place that truly makes a tourist believe that, no matter where you are, people are the same all over. The dining options are minimal, limited to crudités and fresh fruit, but who can look cool and youthful munching a meal in a cocktail lounge? **$$**
64 Kahntuk Cobble

Say Dehkhep (Three Tens) This neighborhood pub has a comfortable smoking room in the back, where it has the feel of those Victorian dinners where the ladies retired to the parlor with their sewing and the gentlemen adjourned to the library for a smoke and a discussion. Somewhat more "middle class" than establishments like Kohnoshuhg Teekudehtoat, Say Dehkhep is quiet but friendly,

and is loved for its sociability and numerous board games. The ale and wine lists are fairly simple, and Say Dehkhep has a few "house brews" among its ales that are well worth a try. This is the kind of establishment to visit to while away the rest of an evening after a satisfying home dining experience. **$**
Number 30 Circle Say East

Tohnentem (The Lake) The location is lovely, the staff is a riot. A serious discussion of philosophy or other issues of import is never allowed to get too ponderous here. The decor features a variety of Atlantean handicrafts, including an impressive sculpted banquette seating area that takes up most of the entire east side of the room. Rather lively for a smoke house, Tohnentem also serves a limited selection of ales, and has a fried root appetizer not unlike an onion ring. **$**
72 Circle Doot West, next to the amphitheater

Gahwindihn (Place of Joy) In the Outer World, Gahwindihn might be the equivalent of a chess club. The subject that occupies the patrons here is not food, drink, or smoke, but the intricacies and strategies of an Atlantean variation of the game of chess. Milo Thatch is said to have spurred the resurgence of interest in this game, which has in turn bred a generation of zealots who gather here nightly to match skills. The room is unremarkable, the menu limited, the smoke is actually minimal. At Gahwindihn, the game's the thing! **$**
16 Circle Kuht, follow the sidewalk around to the left of the old monorail entrance

The Smoke House Although this establishment has something of a shady past (it is rumored to have been a meeting place for the small criminal element that flourished in Atlantis shortly before and after the Cataclysm), it only adds character to this inviting, almost cave-like smoke house. Quite possibly the first such location in Atlantis, it is located downstairs in one of the once-grand citadels "up the hill." Famous for its garlic cheese bread. **$**
44 Coral, just off Circle Dihn

ATLANTIS IN BRIEF

OVERVIEW

DINING

LODGING

NIGHTLIFE & ARTS

SHOPPING

TOURS

PHRASES

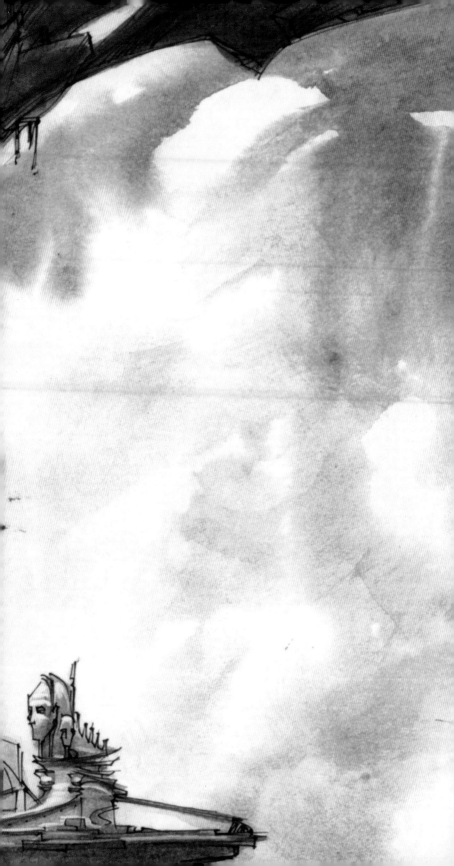

The Deep Sea Exploration Submarine
Ulysses

Crew: 201

Length: 382 feet

Speed: 19 knots

Weight: 18,750 tons (in dry dock)

Armament: twelve torpedo launchers, each with
120 DH-11 high explosive proximity torpedoes.
Launchers have 180 degrees of movement.
22 independently launched attack subpods.

Propulsion:
Primary – four Main SG-18 steam turbines.
Two shafts. 36,000 horsepower
Secondary – Hi-efficiency rechargeable batteries
with twelve hours of emergency power.

Commissioned: 1914

Composition: Made from hybrid galvanized iron alloy
exclusively developed by Whitmore Industries.

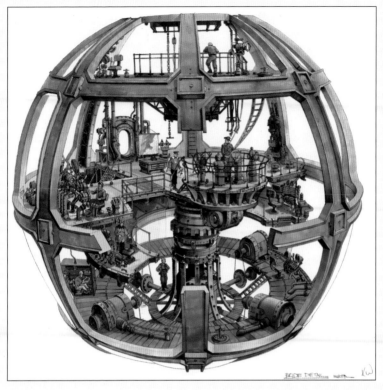

The Ulysses incorporates many advanced technologies not found in any other civilian or military vehicle. It was developed by Whitmore Industries for the sole purpose of finding the lost city of Atlantis. Everything on the Ulysses is overbuilt and meant to survive the extremes of any situation it might encounter.

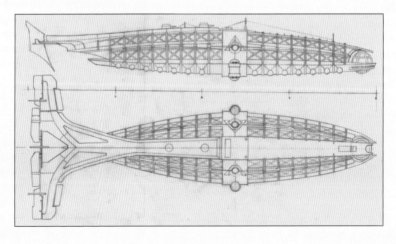

Vehicles
Atlantean

Many of these unique vehicles, no longer having a consistent military application, are available for hire. Milo Thatch taught the Atlanteans to reactivate them, and they are now they are used for tourism, transport, shipping, and commerce. The crystal-powered flying fish are made of an Atlantean substance that is still unknown on the surface world. Their source of locomotion is likely based on magnetic resistance fields caused by the Crystal.

Note: These rides can be frightening for small children, especially excursions that leave the main Atlantis grotto and venture into the surrounding caves.

Martag

Length: 7.83 kelim
Weight: 7.42 nayut
Top speed: 323 wokanos
Crew: 1-2

The Martag is the primary Atlantean attack aircraft. Shaped like a piranha, it is small, maneuverable and is armed with a powerful beam weapon. As all Atlantean vehicles do, the Martag looks like a stone statue when inactive.

Baylokh   Length: 16 kelim
Weight: 11 nayut
Top speed: 308 wokanos
Crew: 1

All Atlantean vehicles derive their
shapes from sea creatures;
the Baylokh takes its shape
from the manta ray.

Kraken   Length: 21 kelim
Weight: 21 nayut
Top speed: 308 wokanos
Crew: 3

The Kraken derives its shape from the squid, with nine
tentacles that can grasp (and crush objects).

Ketak   Length: 5 kelim
Weight: 1.7 nayut
Top speed: 115 wokanos
Crew: 2

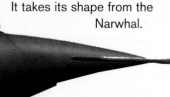

The Ketak is a low-level airborne scooter, used mainly
for nonmilitary personal transport. Its shape is based
on that of a flying fish.

Nartak   Length: 47.83 kelim (not including tusk)
Weight: 31.28 nayut (empty)
Top speed: 285 wokanos
Crew: 2, up to 25 passengers

The Nartak is an airborne transport vehicle, and the
only unarmed Atlantean vehicle. It is primarily used
as a transport craft for troops and supplies.
It takes its shape from the
Narwhal.

Turtak
Length: 8.26 kelim
Weight: 13.79 nayut
Top speed: 308 wokanos
Crew: 3-5

An airborne attack craft, the Turtak takes its shape from the sea turtle.

Martak
Length: 10.4 kelim
(not including antennae)
Weight: 12.73 nayut
Top speed: 292 wokanos in air;
 89 wokanos on land
Crew: 2

An airborne attack craft, the Martak is shaped like a crab, and doubles as a mobile ground vehicle.

Aktirak
Length: 14.3 kelim
Weight: 19 nayut
Top speed: 323 wokanos
Crew: 1-2

An airborne attack craft, the Aktirak is shaped like a hammerhead shark, and was typically piloted by the troop commander.

Rakuda
Length: 20.4 kelim
Weight: 21.21 nayut
Top speed: 285 wokanos
Crew: 5

An airborne attack craft, the Rakuda is a multiperson craft shaped like a barracuda.

Comfortable Lodging
Being a Recommendation of the Accommodations of Atlantis

The uniqueness and variety of accommodations available in Atlantis often amaze visitors. While unusual when compared to the lodgings available in any other major city, there is nothing to compare anywhere on (or in) Earth.

While there is a range of accommodations and prices to suit any taste and bankroll, many visitors choose to "sample" the available lodgings: a typical hotel one evening, an inn the next, then a floating lodge, followed by a private home. It simply depends on the mood and disposition of the tourist. (It may better suit the more tentative visitor to establish a "home base" at a more traditional hotel on their first visit, before venturing to any of the more exotic locales.)

Reservations are strongly recommended for any of the accommodations listed below, and can be made through your Whitmore Industries representative. If you are in Atlantis and decide to try out one of the lodgings for a night or two during your visit, you may also make reservations through the main Nehsettem Wehgehnohsuhg in the city center (immediately south of the Central Wehsertem), or at one of the branch offices located in each city circle, east and west.

Guide to Ratings

$$$$	More than $200	$$	$50-100
$$$	$100-200	$	Less than $50

All prices for a standard double room or equivalent during peak season

ATLANTIS IN BRIEF

OVERVIEW

DINING

LODGING

NIGHTLIFE & ARTS

SHOPPING

TOURS

PHRASES

BED AND BREAKFAST LODGING

As with the native dining custom, lodging is mostly of the bed-and-breakfast style, with several of the accommodations provided in family homes. This again offers the visitor a variety of experiences in a variety of dwellings and, although somewhat unusual to Outer World tastes, is one of the best ways to truly experience Atlantis. For those interested in encountering a variety of Atlantean architecture, decor, customs, cuisine, and personalities, this is the way to go. The following are the most prominent of the Atlantean guest houses:

Burroughs House Hugging a hillside and veritably encased in lush vegetation, Burroughs House began its life as a small bungalow retreat. Over the years, it has been enlarged and added to, creating a cozy and accommodating destination. The *en suite* apartment that is the primary guest room feels to Outer Worlders a bit like staying in the Swiss Family Robinson's exotic tree house. The host residents are youthful and vigorous, and given to lively discussion and late nights around the dining table. A *very* old one-eyed cat named Odin is the house "mascot." This is H.G. Wells's favorite haunt on his visits to Atlantis. (The house is named for Edgar Rice Burroughs, the author of *Tarzan of the Apes*, who has become one of the most frequent celebrity visitors to Atlantis.) **$$**
29 Pinehurst Road in Circle Kut West

Madison House Markuh and Kahrell are a gregarious and intelligent married couple who love nothing more than hosting friends in their home and modestly preparing some of the most outstanding meals you will ever have. Their house is warm and traditional with an edge of stylish decor, and the guest rooms are in a private *en suite* lower level. Markuh is also a well-known Atlantean craftsman; his carpentry is much sought after. The dog, Carla, is part of the family, so expect a cold nose with your warm greeting. The house was named for frequent visitor Lewis (Madison) Terman, (1877-), the educational psychologist and Stanford University professor (1910-).

Informally known as "Madison," Terman has coined the term "IQ" ("Intelligence Quotient") and has developed intelligence tests, including the recent Stanford-Binet intelligence test published in *The Measurement of Intelligence* (1916). **$$$**

27 Alki Road in Circle Shah West

Kirkhweishaus If your destination is *fun*, then the house of Atlantean artist and eccentric Kirkhweis is where you should head. The accommodations are ample and comfortable (with a decor that is a fascinating destination in and of itself), and the intelligent, soft-spoken Kirkhweis loves to receive visitors. Expect long discussions with lots of laughter, and be forewarned your host is quite learned and insatiably curious about anything to do with the Outer World — expect to be queried about *every* aspect of Outer World life. Throughout the public areas, visitors will find the owner's art and handcrafts on display. If you're looking for fun spots or interesting Atlantis tours, Kirkhweis can direct you to destinations throughout the lost empire that will suit you to a tee. (Sometimes it feels as if an Atlantean destination recommended by Kirkhweis has been created just to suit your need!) **$$$**

500 Buenavista Street, at Alahmeeduh

The Library  Circle Doot Library, like a sort of monastery of librarians, remains much the same as it was just after the Cataclysm. Despite its ascetic origins, the accommodations are surprisingly warm and inviting, and are a fascinating representation of the building's functional evolution from athenaeum to domicile. For a detailed history of the site, see Museums. There is no food service in The Library (naturally), but there is a coffee bar/bakery in the plaza outside, and there are several dining options within a few minutes' walk. **$$**

30 Circle Doot North, across from the old monorail station

TRADITIONAL HOTELS

If a traditional hotel is more to your liking, there are options for such accommodation up the hill. Here are the few "four-star" resorts that Atlantis has to offer. These tend to be rather staid and quiet, since they are so off the beaten path of the general population of the city. If an exotic and indulgent retreat is what you have in mind, there are none better than these.

Atlantean Grand Hotel This beautifully refurbished pre-Cataclysm palace gives the visitor a good idea what the tourist in ancient Atlantis probably experienced. Breathtaking architecture with vaulted and coffered ceilings, huge and majestic public rooms, exquisite finishes and furnishings, and unending facilities and amenities — the term "grand" is an understatement. The finest of the hand arts that the ancients could create abound within these walls. The hotel features spacious, well-appointed rooms, each with a private white-marble bathroom and recently updated with all modern plumbing and "climate control" machinery. Peht Zoldt, whose gracious service is the standard in Atlantean hospitality, sets the pace for the crack concierge staff.

Although travelers may feel that hotel restaurants lack the panache of other dining spots, **The Garden Court Restaurant** is an exception, featuring a weekly wine tasting and exceptional live entertainment. And the garden isn't just a name: the atrium overflows with a bounty of native Atlantean flora. There is an up-to-date **gymnasium**, which the management quaintly terms a "health club," and the **wehsertem** of the Atlantean Grand Hotel provides a shopping area that is, like its host hotel, more refined, staid, and traditional than other Atlantean sites of commerce. (There is also one of Atlantis's two 24-hour **pharmacies** here, specializing in crystal healing and the abundantly available herbal tonics, poultices, and remedies that are a specialty of Atlantean medicine.)
78 rooms and suites with bath **$$$$**
14 Circle Dihn North

Trous Dale Plaza For an exotic and indulgent retreat, the Trous Dale Plaza has recently risen to great prominence, particularly among harried Outer Worlders in need of complete escape. The creation of one of Atlantis's most renowned artisans, gregarious, bearded, redheaded Gahrée (a native of the mountain village of Trous), the philosophy of the Trous Dale Plaza is to bring the peace, serenity, and comfort of one of the owner's native dells into the bustling cityscape.

The Plaza has been configured from a grouping of adjacent buildings from several periods of Atlantean history. The reception house is a grand arrival point, with an airy, oak-beamed lobby and an efficient arrangement of guest services. The rooms are contained within separate outer buildings, which gives a sense of privacy to your stay. The rooms themselves are big and clean, with a muted, relaxing decor that adds to the sense of peace and order here.

Your host also enjoys communicating by *drawing*, so expect much of the communication with your host to be in the form of clever cartoons you'll find on your pillow, guest room door, or bathroom mirror. The grounds are exquisitely and exotically landscaped, there are serenity gardens, fountains, pools, and other examples of the native surroundings of Trous tucked away throughout the property.

The spa amenities are the core of the Trous Dale Plaza. Anything a guest requires — from a simple haircut to massages and herbal and crystal treatments — is available from a serene and cheerful staff. The Plaza also features an excellent line of aromatic cosmetics and lotions for sale. A superb in-house **restaurant** serves healthy repasts based on fruits, vegetables, and grains. Beware — meat and even seafood are the exception rather than the rule here, but there are excellent soups every day.
48 rooms and suites with bath $$$$
14 Circle Doot West

ATLANTIS IN BRIEF

OVERVIEW

DINING

LODGING

NIGHTLIFE & ARTS

SHOPPING

TOURS

PHRASES

Kehloabtem Mahkijtuhg (The King's Chamber) How many people have dreamed of going to an exotic foreign land and staying in the King's Palace? One of the many wonders of Atlantis is the ability to do just that at the Kehloabtem Mahkijtuhg in the Nedakh Palace complex. Still occupied by Queen Kida and members of the Royal Court and Royal Family, a wing of the palace was recently opened as overnight accommodation. Architecturally peerless, the Palace represents the true sovereign of pre-Cataclysm design and elegance.

The gigantic guest rooms are richly adorned with pre-Cataclysm sculpture and furniture designed by top artisans, but contain all the modern amenities. Many have adjoining balconies with spectacular views of the city below and the largest suite boasts an opulent oricalcum-plated bathtub. Extra touches include netting over the beds (a must in evading the humid climate's buzzing bugs) and dining areas lit by firefly lanterns.

Not surprisingly, the food service here, although pricey, is exceptional — even royal. There is no restaurant (the Royal Dining Hall is private) so all food service is brought directly to the rooms. *18 rooms with bath* **$$$$**
Number One Center Circle Dihn

The Armory The name of this hotel derives from its building's original function: this was the first Atlantean armory. Tucked on a leafy corner in Circle Dihn, the Armory has massive walls which guarantee guest accommodations of utter peace and quiet. The staff is friendly and attentive, and the guest rooms are richly furnished with pre-Cataclysm Atlantean antiques and art works. Rooms without private bath are half-price.

Although the Armory lacks a "destination attraction" like the restaurant and shopping of the Atlantean Grand or the spa amenities of the Trous Dale Plaza, there are many details of note for the attentive visitor. The building was actually built around its own central waterfall, which provides an odd serenity to a building created for such a military function. Pre-Cataclysm mosaic floors of shifting hues and iridescence veritably flow throughout the entire building. Note the frescoes within the vaulting in the ceiling of the massive **dining room**, where traditional Atlantean dishes are served to hotel guests and an appreciative native population, too.

38 rooms, most with private bath **$$$$**
37 Circle Dihn North

INNS, PUBS, AND LODGES

For many, the experience of travel is not remote, but kinetic, and their desire is to eschew the tourist traps and experience the destination. If that is the case, the only real place to be is in one of the smaller inns, pubs, or lodges located by the water.

Kehloabtem Wehsertem (Marketplace Inn) The friendly owners of this family-run inn go out of their way to make you feel welcome. The large, spotless rooms are a bargain at twice the price, and the location in the heart of the lively marketplace/bazaar of the Waterfront Wehsertem, although a bit noisy at times, offers exceptional convenience to dining, shopping, and activities.

15 rooms with private baths **$**
90 Shoreline Drive, across from Wehgehnohsuhg

Behnwehston Standard rooms and service and a central location make this small inn well worth considering. The neighborhood offers a decent range of dining, easy access to other sectors of the city, and picturesque strolls along the water. Slee, the proprietress of Behnweston, is a connoisseur of fine clothes and costumery, and many examples of priceless pre-Cataclysm Atlantean Royal wardrobe from her collection are gorgeously displayed here. The petite and feisty Slee is also an aficionado of Outer World science fiction literature, which may explain why H.G. Wells is a frequent visitor to this house.

6 rooms with private baths **$$**
40 Jahksen Road at Cuhlvar in Circle Kut West

Pension Atlantis Comfortable (if not exactly luxurious), clean, and friendly, the Pension Atlantis is well run and extremely affordable. A relatively new establishment, the clientele consists mostly of young natives away for a holiday and Outer Worlders trying to save a few dollars. It is close to the aquarium and zoo, and central to most of the waterfront nightlife. Before the fall, the spartan rooms of Pension Atlantis actually served as interrogation cells for the Atlantean Secret Police!
15 rooms, most with private bath **$**
56 Aurora Road, near the Kan-Lis moorage

The Falls Lodge The Falls Lodge is a floating hotel, located in the midst of several other floating businesses. The Falls offers the peace and coziness of an alpine lodge (the building is constructed of stout hewn logs) but with the gentle, relaxing motion of the water beneath. The dark-wood building has only seven rooms, but the intimacy makes for unparalleled service, particularly for such an inexpensive and unique establishment.
7 rooms with baths **$$**
47 Shoreline (take the barrel-float gangway)

Pewhud This intimate little inn is built within the walls of a pre-Cataclysm public building, with ornately carved and burnished bas-reliefs of ancient Atlantean life, a spacious terrazzo lobby, and seventeen richly and comfortably furnished rooms. But sometimes a place simply cannot escape its point of origin. It just happens that in its original state, the building was a public toilet (the name *Pewhud* is actually Atlantean for "toilet"). For years, the owners tried to persuade the population to refer to this gem of an inn by its new name (an Atlantean term meaning "Gone Away"), but finally decided, "if you can't beat 'em, join 'em," and started calling their own business The Toilet, too. Local musicians congregate in the tap room most evenings.
18 rooms with baths **$$**
12 Circle Dihn East, next to the temple square

Teegul Wehsertem (Marketplace Haven) Located in the heart of the bustling marketplace/bazaar of the Central Wehsertem, this lodge was once the heart of the Atlantis theater community. It has seen some hard times, but new owners are working hard to restore its former luster in appearance, service, and sociability. Until then, the tight, tidy rooms, friendly staff (many of them actors and performers), and fin de siècle charm are reason enough to recommend it.
24 rooms, most with private bath **$$**
22 Circle Doot West, near the Schu-Macherr Theater

Donnelly's Inn Another of the barge-built inns, this is a handsome, efficient lodging with clean, spacious accommodations at a fair rate. Although somewhat plain in comparison to many of its competitors, for the explorer who likes a no-nonsense room where the main activity is sleep, this place is quiet, comfortable, and well run by a courteous staff. The small "footing" provided by the barge has dictated an almost whimsical vertical construction. The inn was named for the famed Atlantologist Ignatius Donnelly, the renowned taproom is known as Blavatsky's.
12 rooms with bath **$$**
11 Aurora Shore, south gangway

Nightlife and the Arts

Being a Tutorial of the Lost City's Evening Amusements and Cultural Institutions

The traditions of the Outer World exist to varying degrees within Atlantean culture, and the eagle-eyed visitor can find modes of socialization, celebration, culture, and craft.

NIGHTLIFE

Cabaret The one and only Atlantean performer who truly fits the mold of what we know as a "cabaret" performer is the inimitable Shadehm, a sort of grand, eccentric, and charming "Auntie Mame," who entertains with a combination of Atlantean standards, torch songs, and bawdy ditties that must have come to her eons ago from the sailors of the ancient Atlantean seaport (23 Beekman Place). Also try **Ohbehsuhg Kehloabtem** (Lava Room, *64 Kahntuk Cobble, in the basement*) the Atlantean equivalent of a small Manhattan lounge where the entertainment varies, but tends toward keyboard and vocalists crooning Atlantean pop standards.

Music Clubs Music is everywhere in Atlantis, and a few of the talented musicians and vocalists gather together to play, sing, experiment musically, and enjoy one another's talents. Luckily for you, they do so where you are invited to watch and listen. The most popular such gathering place is the taproom of **Pewhud** *(12 Circle Dihn East, next to the temple square)*. Music starts around 9:00 PM, but come earlier to get a seat.

Pubs, Bars and Lounges "Bars" or "lounges" as we know them are not traditional fixtures of Atlantis. Social life of the drinking variety usually takes place in pubs, which are located in neighborhoods throughout the city. Tourists are welcome to join in the evening ritual of sitting around tables, talking, sometimes smoking (not a terribly typical habit here), and drinking the fine and varied ales of

Atlantis. Before venturing in though, here are a few points of pub etiquette: Always ask if a chair is occupied before sitting down. To order an ale, do not wave the waiter down or call out for his attention, he will usually assume that you want an ale and deliver it to you without being asked. To refuse, simply shake your head and say, "no, thank you." At the end of the evening, the waiter will tally up with you. Some of the more popular pubs are **Kohnoshuhg Teekudehtoat** *(34 Circle Doot North)* the "artist's" pub **PagoPago** *(45 Alahmeeduh Avenue)*, **Say Dehkhep** *(Number 30 Circle Say East)*, and **Tohnentem** *(72 Circle Doot West, next to the small amphitheater)*.

The major hotels also offer a somewhat more sedate kind of evening entertainment, usually of the "piano and port wine" variety, and require a somewhat more elevated dress code. For details, check with the concierge at the **Atlantean Grand Hotel** *(14 Circle Dihn North)*, **Trous Dale Plaza** *(14 Circle Doot West)*, or **The Armory** *(37 Circle Dihn North)*.

THE ARTS

Atlantis's cultural panache is the stuff of legend, and the citizenry's love of the arts insures that tickets are usually booked far in advance by Atlanteans. The concierge at your lodging may be able to obtain tickets, or check the Nehsettem Wehgehnohsuhg in the city center, immediately south of the Central Wehsertem, or one of the branch offices located in each city circle, east and west. Otherwise, there are usually at least a few tickets at the venue box office immediately before a performance.

Theater Like any civilization, the Atlanteans have developed thriving arts. Theater is largely created with children in mind, with an emphasis on puppet or costume character shows. The most prominent puppet showman in Atlantis is Schu Macherr, whose breathtaking presentations are critically acclaimed and award winning. His theater, the **Animateum** *(32 Circle Say West)*, is a whimsical venue located in one of the newer buildings in Circle Say, a structure shaped like a giant peaked cap. Check the Nehsettem Wehgehnohsuhg for what is being performed and when, but be forewarned, these programs are frequently sold out.

The Animateum has a second stage, where popular shows can be moved or more experimental programs can be developed. It is named after the Atlantean ventriloquist Jahri MaHo-nee, a long time friend and colleague of Schu Macherr.

Music Music is a staple of Atlantean culture — in fact, visitors have often referred to the innate "musicality" of Atlantis. Street musicians are naturally in abundance, but they play for the love of music and the desire to share it with others, not for money — so *do not* drop money or coins near them, as they will be offended.

Concerts are held throughout the city all year long. The two most prominent venues include the **Amphitheater** *(70 Circle Doot West)*, and the **Royal Opera House** *(Number One Center Circle Dihn)*. The Amphitheater houses a pleasant outdoor performance space with an informal air, the audience usually brings picnic dinners and wine to enjoy with the program. A more formal concert venue, only recently resurrected from the ruins is the magnificent pre-Cataclysm Royal Opera House which, with 2,500 seats and standing room, is the largest such indoor venue in the city. (Well, most of it is indoors, it should be noted, since its restoration will be many years in completion, but the Atlantean climate makes this acceptable.) The behavior and dress at this venue is somewhat more formal than that of the Amphitheater.

Concerts are also held in the gardens of the **Atlantis Zoological Park** *(Number One Center Circle Dihn)*. As with other arts, check the Nehsettem Wehgehnohsuhg for what program is being performed and when.

Dance
Dance as a performance art can be seen in the venues described above. Occasionally, you may see a spontaneous performance or witness a rehearsal or ritual in one of the public parks or gardens throughout the city. Dancers tend to congregate and "workshop" their choreography in **The Meadows** *(part of the Nedakh Palace complex, Number One Center Circle Dihn)*.

Monthly social dances are a much-anticipated event, as much for their performance and audience appreciation as for their social nature. Check with your lodging host, concierge, or the Nehsettem Wehgehnohsuhg for what is being performed and when, or for the dates of the monthly citywide dance.

Museums
The history of Atlantis makes for a fascinating exploration for those so inclined. Several new museums and libraries have been established in the past few years and are well worth seeking out. Of special interest is the **Atlantis Museum of History and Industry** *(67 Circle Shah West)*, which has been established by Milo J. Thatch in a disused Atlantean industrial building and features a comprehensive display of Atlantean artifacts from ancient times to the Whitmore Expedition. Often Thatch himself is on hand to deliver an address or simply to meet with visitors and discuss his great fascination, Atlantis!

After the Cataclysm, the king ordered all accounts of history to be destroyed and the population of Atlantis lost track of their once great history. There was a small cadre of bibliophiles, however, who rescued many of the Atlantean libraries, public and private, and squirreled them away in the old **Circle Doot**

Library *(30 Circle Doot North, across from the old monorail station)* and tried to maintain a focus of study on their contents. Like a sort of "monastery of librarians," they eventually took up rooms and became residents as well as caretakers here. The building is classic ancient Atlantean, and in addition to being a reference library has become a popular lodging place.

HANDICRAFTS

As long lived as Atlanteans are, quite a few of them have developed quite extensive artistic skills. Hence, the Atlantean art scene is rich and varied, with all manner of painting, textile work, metallurgy, sculpture, and glasswork on display in museums and galleries within the city. Often, the sincere act of appreciation of an artisan's skills will result in the gift of a beautiful rarity. But if the tourist expects such generosity, they will find naught but rejection.

Sculpture  **Carving** is their favorite medium, with wood being the most common. A typical wood carving (usually of figures or animals or combinations of the two) will take three to five years to complete. **Stonework** is for the more advanced sculptor, and **metalwork and casting** is reserved for only the masters of the craft. After a successful casting is made – when the mold is broken open – the entire neighborhood turns out to watch. There are parties and feasting and all the local shops close in celebration.

Tapestries and Textiles The textiles of Atlantis are exquisitely wrought; many made from native silks. The Atlantean weavers are truly the finest known, and like their brother carvers, have developed exquisite skills due to their lengthy life spans.

There is practically nowhere in Atlantis where a visitor cannot view or experience Atlantean art and handicraft. Check with your lodging host, concierge, or the Nehsettem Wehgehnohsuhg for any new or noteworthy artists or installations, or to reserve space on the special **Artisans of Atlantis** tour.

ATLANTIS IN BRIEF

OVERVIEW

DINING

LODGING

NIGHTLIFE & ARTS

SHOPPING

TOURS

PHRASES

Satisfying Shopping

Being a Register of Recommended Merchants of Atlantean Crafts, Goods, Merchandise and Keepsakes

Although the indigenous fashions of Atlantis will not make the city a rival for the haute couture of Paris or Rome, there is still much to value in a shopping trip here. Atlantean shops and craftsmen abound, and for those who prize a shopping trip the way an explorer loves an expedition, Atlantis offers the greatest satisfaction of all. Shopping in Atlantis is a rare and fulfilling process of exploration, education, and barter.

SHOPPING DISTRICTS

The major shopping areas in Atlantis are the three **Wehsertem**, or markets. These are large, varied emporia that have evolved over many centuries, branching haphazardly from key entrances. Neophyte visitors often get lost in the Wehsertem — which is quite honestly the best way to experience their variety and abundance.

Central Wehsertem is located in the city center, and abounds with fresh meats and fish, fruits and vegetables, baked goods, dairy products and cheeses, flowers, and of course, practical objects and arts and crafts.

The companion market, the **Waterfront Wehsertem**, is slightly smaller and more labyrinthine and gritty, but with more and fresher bounty of the sea, and the unpolished charm and frankness of a child.

For those interested in a more conventional shopping experience, the **Wehsertem** of the **Atlantean Grand Hotel** is, like its host hotel, more refined, staid, and traditional.

Department Stores
: There are only two department stores in Atlantis, neither of which would make Mr. Wanamaker or Mr. Macy terribly jealous. Clean, efficient, and friendly, with a nice variety of stock from simple housewares to clothing, **Puknohl Brothers & Sons** (54 Marietta Street) is expedient if not terribly interesting shopping. **Wandehm & Bendoh** (22 Alki Road) features more luxury items and boutique foods, but is similarly conventional.

Street Markets Before dawn each day, several pushcarts leave the three Wehsertem to "set up shop" in various neighborhoods throughout the city. For daily fresh fruits, vegetables, seafood, meats and dairy, these pushcarts constitute the "neighborhood store." For more varied goods, or to make such purchases later in the day, it is necessary to go to the Wehsertem.

The best market for nonfoods is a sort of flea market of clothing, objects, curios, and such *(Circle Doot North, a few hundred yards east of Kohnoshuhg Teekudehtoat).* An Atlantean version of London's Portobello Road, it has evolved over many years along a collapsed stretch of track near the central platform of the old municipal monorail system. Arrive early, as the bargains disappear quickly, and the stands, tents, and carts tend to disperse by mid-afternoon.

SPECIALTY STORES

Antiques Atlanteans have little appreciation for their "antiques" as such, since they still use so many of their pre-Cataclysm things in daily life. There are a few boutiques that specialize in hand objects and bibelots of the ancient kind, but no "antiques shops" as they are known in the Outer World. (Besides, I'd like to see you convince your Whitmore Industries representative to haul the stunning armoire you've just found up the Carlsbad Cavern fissure.) **Roknah** *(64 Kahntuk Cobble)* has a nice variety of Atlantean utensils, dinnerware, cups, glasses, and cutlery. **Hantan & Daughters** *(21 Pinehurst Road in Circle Kut West)* has a fun collection of hand objects like mirrors, combs, powder boxes, and paperweights.

Woodcarvings The lush forests of Atlantis provide exceptional materials for the carver's craft. Since only a limited number of hard and soft woods from the harvest are set aside for carving (in a well-designed effort not to deplete the area's raw materials), and the carvings themselves can take as long to develop as the original components, wood carvings are cherished treasures. **Puknohl Brothers & Sons** (54 Marietta Street) has a small but exceptional Wood Crafts department.

Sculpture and Castings Stonework is for the more advanced sculptor. Metalwork and casting are reserved for only the masters of the craft. Some of the smaller sculptures and hand objects can be purchased as gift or souvenir items by Outer Worlders in the same venues as the wood and stone work described above. Please note that during the parties and feast that follow the successful breaking open of a casting, local shops are closed.

Visitors can take some of the smaller sculptures and hand objects home. The wood carver's tools are crafted with as much ornamentation and design as the carvings, and are often available for purchase. Artisans of all varieties can be found selling wares of their own making off barrows and pushcarts in the neighborhood markets or in stands, tents, and carts in the three Wehsertem. Otherwise, **Karadekh & Co.** (12 Marietta Street) carries an ample selection of sculpture for sale.

Tapestries and Textiles The textiles of Atlantis are exquisitely wrought; many made from native silks. Like their brother carvers, Atlantean weavers developed fine skills due to their lengthy life spans. Patterns based on local flora and fauna, crystal configurations and tattoo symbology are among the most popular, depicted in strong, vibrant colors. Weavers can usually be found selling their own creations from stalls and carts in the Wehsertem and the neighborhood markets. They have even been known to give shoppers the clothes off their backs at the right price. **The Atlantean Grand Hotel** (12 Circle Dihn North) has an excellent textile boutique, as does the department store **Wandehm & Bendoh** (22 Alki Road).

ATLANTIS IN BRIEF

OVERVIEW

DINING

LODGING

NIGHTLIFE & ARTS

SHOPPING

TOURS

PHRASES

Food Specialties Sweets and candied fruits are special treats. Both **The Atlantean Grand Hotel** *(12 Circle Dihn North)* and **Wandehm & Bendoh** *(22 Alki Road)* have exceptional food boutiques, but decent products can also be found in each of the three Wehsertem. Some of the unique Atlantean food specialties have been put up for transport back to the Outer World, although they tend to be quite expensive. Be warned: the popular "squid tentacle on a stick" does not preserve or transport well. It is a treat that should only be enjoyed fresh from an Atlantean vendor.

Floral Atlantis abounds with beautiful flowers, and many Outer Worlders have commented on the unique floral arrangements they see in many of the lobbies and public spaces of Atlantis businesses. These are the work of Ken-Noth and his **Villa Caprice Floral Design Studio** *(1602 Dehxtar Road)*. Although some say the decidedly Italian name came from an ancient sailor, Ken-Noth actually credits Outer World author (and Atlantis habitue) Elizabeth Enright with naming his business. Cut flowers and plants are available in abundance off barrows and pushcarts in the neighborhood markets or in stands, tents, and carts in the three Wehsertem.

Tattoo Parlors Tattoos have been known in many countries, cultures, and ages, and many of these may owe their origins to the Tattoo Artists of Atlantis. The bestowal of tattoos is part of significant and ancient ritual, and as the Atlanteans demonstrate courage or statesmanship they are granted more and different significant tattoos. Ultimately, the rank of an Atlantean can be determined by "reading" their body art. (For instance, the late king had more tattoos than any other citizen due to his centuries of courage, wisdom, service, and statesmanship.)

"Greenhorn Tattoos," essentially souvenirs for visitors, can be applied by the Royal Tattooist, **Inky Neshak**, in his tiny studio outside the

Nedakh Palace complex *(on the Aviary side at Number Ten Center Circle Dihn)*.

Fun Things for Children Children enjoy the beautifully made watercolor and colored chalk sets available widely throughout Atlantis. Many stores also offer unique wooden toys, sure to delight any youngster. There is a marvelous toy store in **The Atlantean Grand Hotel** *(12 Circle Dihn North)*, and **Hantan & Daughters** *(21 Pinehurst Road in Circle Kut West)* has a very interesting selection of objects for the young and young at heart.

Atlantean Crystal Although abundant, Atlantean Crystal is considered sacred and is absolutely *not* for sale. It is essential to the livelihood and endurance of the Atlanteans and Atlantis, yet everyone has a shard and the crystal is a common sight. Oddly, it is *given* freely, but it is a highly prized gift, and its bestowal should never be anticipated.

Tours and Destinations

Being a Conspectus of Various Destination Journeys Available to the Atlantis Visitor

In addition to the sights, sounds, and locales of the bustling urban Atlantis, there are a variety of other points of interest, destinations, historical sites, and fascinating byways available to the Atlantis visitor.

Whether your interest is history, architecture, vegetation and foliage, or wildlife, there are many tours and destinations beyond the hotels, restaurants, shopping, and recreation available in the central city.

Nehsettem Wehgehnohsuhg (Traveler's Office) sponsors several tours of the city, for residents and visitors from the Outer World. Schedule varies according to demand, so be sure to check for the specific tour or destination that you desire. Day tourists should always make this their first stop for general tour information, updates on weather and travel conditions, and detailed maps.

Nehsettem Wehgehnohsuhg is located in the city center, immediately south of the Central Wehsertem, with branch offices located in each city circle, east and west.

Here are a few of the most recommended tours and sites of Atlantis (note that all of these attractions are free):

The Royal Palace Tour While a wing of the Nedakh Palace Complex has been opened to the public to serve as overnight accommodation (see Kehloabtem Mahkijtuhg, under Lodging), most tourists come there for the famed Royal Palace Tour, an "on the inside" look into Atlantean Royalty. The complex in its heyday included luxurious private apartments for the royal family, an extensive library (which was largely destroyed after the Cataclysm), and the recreational court where a game called "dunok" was played with a ball made from the hide of cave bats (*dunok tinemoshep* in Atlantean, hence the name *dunok*).

Historical Atlantis A three-hour Historical Atlantis tour is offered year-round, and combines walking, watercraft, and hover-vehicle views of the majestic city, guided by an informed and informative Atlantean docent. This tour is an especially thorough primer for the uninitiated; for the more knowledgeable visitor, this enlightening excursion will help separate fact from fiction — and may turn some of your long-accepted truths into legends.

Architectural Atlantis  This tour and the Artisans of Atlantis tour were created and are run by the same people who created the Historical Atlantis tour above. This tour features smaller groups, more specific subject matter, and more personal interaction with the locales and citizenry. It combines walking, watercraft, and hover-vehicle transportation in an overview of the different architectural styles and eras of Atlantean building history, and glimpses into several Atlantis buildings that are otherwise unavailable.

Artisans of Atlantis This tour features smaller groups, more specific subject matter, and more personal interaction with the locals and citizenry. It combines walking, watercraft, and hover-vehicle transportation in an overview of the many different arts and handicrafts of Atlantis, their history, a tour of several of the best extant examples, and personal demonstrations by several of the finest artisans in Atlantis.

The *Ulysses* Memorial  Located in the underground air pocket where the original expedition survivors surfaced, the Memorial was erected and dedicated by Preston Whitmore himself, to commemorate the heroism of the crew of the *Ulysses*, the deep-sea exploration submarine that was years ahead of its time (see sidebar). The exhibit includes artifacts from the original expedition, uniforms of the original explorers, and the actual tail section of the sub, which was towed to the site by Whitmore Industries crews to take its position as the centerpiece of the exhibit (and quite

frankly in an effort to remove any evidence of the Whitmore Expedition from the floor of the ocean!)

Also a part of the grotto is an elaborate carved entry portal that leads to a spectacular section of early Atlantean highway. (Note that there are no surface connections from this site, visitors must return to the crossroads to connect with the surface exits through Carlsbad Caverns and Mammoth Caves.)

Along the Atlantean Highway On the ancient highway approaching Atlantis, there is occasional evidence of visitors from the Outer World. Most explorers did not make it very far into the tunnels and fissures that lead to Atlantis, and many of the ancient entrances are now under water. There are, however, a few wonderful archaeological sites that bear evidence of early Roman and Nordic forays into the underground labyrinth that leads to Atlantis. The Roman site has an ancient helmet and several other fascinating artifacts on display.

The road to Atlantis is well known for its portals — a series of traps or obstacles created to thwart unwanted visitors and discourage further exploration. The wind tunnel in the Bahodmok region is one such amazing site of Atlantean engineering and is famous as a breeding ground of the Bahodmok tigers. The site features a virtual forest of carved stone columns and faces, most of which are actually hollow. When the pressure in the tunnel changes due to surface gravitational and geothermal fluctuations, the winds in this sector of the caves can blow in excess of 150 miles per hour. *The Shepherd's Journal* made reference to this phenomenon and warned not only of the excessive winds, but also of the shrill noise emitted from the carved columns and stone heads.

Check local conditions before visiting this site and a guide is always recommended, since visits during windstorms may result in serious personal injury. (Check conditions through your Whitmore Representative, hotel concierge or hospitality staff, or by contacting the Nehsettem Wehgehnohsuhg.)

Cavern Tours In the many centuries since the Cataclysm, the citizens of Atlantis have engaged in extensive exploration of the miles and miles of grottoes, caves, and caverns that surround their city. Some of these explorations were for hunting and food gathering purposes, some were to set up outposts or blockades, or to try to find other civilizations nearby (the Moth Men). They built an elaborate road system, intricately and ornately carved and decorated, sometimes using natural features such as stalactites and stalagmites as part of their structures creating fascinating columns and arches.

Bridges, roads, buildings, temples, tunnels — all of these are scattered throughout the caverns. Most are in a state of advanced disrepair or ruin, as they were built when the Atlanteans still had a strong memory of their time of ascendancy on the surface and were trying to (literally) carve one out down below. The ensuing eons have tumbled, buried, shifted or otherwise altered the remaining catacombs.

This once grand and elaborate system, now fallen into disuse and ruin (and crawling with various underworldly wildlife), makes for one of the most fascinating of all the tours available.

ATLANTIS IN BRIEF

OVERVIEW

DINING

LODGING

NIGHTLIFE & ARTS

SHOPPING

TOURS

PHRASES

The Aziz Archaeological Dig The Aziz Archaeological Dig is well worth the half-day journey required to reach it. Aziz was the shepherd who, according to legend, wrote the fabled *Shepherd's Journal* during an accidental expedition to the lost continent. For many years, it was not clear if Aziz was a true personage or if he was a character whose existence evolved over the centuries. The writing in *The Shepherd's Journal* is all of one hand, but some say the drawings are of a different style.

In any case, there is some archaeological evidence of an ancient campsite of visitors from the outside world. This site in the Tuyeb province includes a prehistoric stone circle, and encampment of what appears to be a single individual. There are cave paintings nearby that appear to be in the same style and hand as those of the artist in the Journal.

Outer Sectors Tour Another popular tour covers the outer sectors of Atlantis. Visitors of all ages will take delight in seeing the Yeragos Province, which is famed for the nesting grounds of an exotic species of semiaquatic bird. Moreover, you should not miss the enclave of formerly submerged murals, mosaics, and frescos that illustrate the history of the Atlantean people and civilization. Tour guides can fully explain the intricacies of the artwork and the stories they contain.

TOURS OF NATURE

Atlantis has an abundant native plant and animal variety. Much of what the visitor will see will seem common; some of it familiar, but with a slightly altered nature; some of it exotic to the point of sheer fantasy.

For anyone who enjoys the typical zoos and wildlife expeditions of the Outer World, the Atlantean equivalents are not to be missed. The aviary, aquarium, arboretum, and zoo are an excellent primer (they are also free), but there are also expeditions and tours that add such erudition and depth that anyone even slightly serious in their study of native flora and fauna should make the time to experience them.

The Aviary The amazing and exotic birds and other creatures of flight are on display within this soaring avian habitat, recently resurrected on the site of the old Royal Dovecote. Restored, repaired, and greatly expanded, the new Atlantis Aviary gets better every day, and is a haven for the feathered and their friends.
Open Daily • Complimentary Admission
Number One Center Circle Dihn

The Aquarium Naturally a culture so eternally bound to the sea has one of the world's most extensive aquariums. Not just a "fish zoo," this is also a habitat, hospital, and research facility. New creatures and exhibits are revealed on what seems to be an almost-daily basis. The Aquarium is also centrally located in the Waterfront district adjacent to the Waterfront Wehsertem.
Open Daily • Complimentary Admission
67 Shoreline Drive

The Arboretum The abundant woods, plants, and wild flowers of Atlantis are cultivated, conserved, and exhibited here. Once a lavish private estate "up the hill," the Arboretum has only recently been rescued from centuries of neglect and overgrowth with the serious commitment of a nascent horticultural community of Atlantis. Although far from complete, their efforts are well worth examining.
Open Daily • Complimentary Admission
Number 28 Center Circle Dihn South

Atlantis Zoological Park and Gardens Like the nearby Aviary, this wondrous and growing collection of creatures was recently reborn from the ruins of the ancient Royal Menagerie. Like the Aquarium, the "zoo" is no longer an "animal display," but is an agency that serves as habitat, hospital, and research facility. It has been expanded to enter and encompass the ancient Royal Gardens, where Atlantean Botanists are now hard at work growing, preserving, and cataloging flower and plant species.
Open Daily • Complimentary Admission
Number One Center Circle Dihn

Guided Cave Bug Hunt Giant cave bugs have been hunted and used for food, clothing, armor, and even building materials. This guided cave bug hunt for the big game enthusiast results not in a kill, however, but is a naturalist hike to observe the habits and habitat of this peculiar creature.

Squid-Bat Spelunking Squid-bats are fairly large animals (about 10 feet across and 15 feet long on average) that resemble jellyfish. The body clings to cave roofs with the tentacles hanging below, looking deceptively like a cluster of stalactites. They live and travel in groups of fifteen to fifty (known as 'convoys'), covering large expanses of cave ceiling. They are carnivorous and convert what they eat into hydrogen, which allows them to float like a hot-air balloon. Needless to say, they don't like flame of any kind, and will not be found anywhere near firefly nests. Squid-Bat Spelunking is another naturalist hike to observe the habits and habitat of these eerie invertebrates.

Beware the Fireflies!
Due to the hot and humid climate, insects abound in Atlantis. The most notable and dangerous are the fireflies. When their nests are threatened, they can heat up and burn anything slightly less flammable than stone.

Lava Whale Hunt The largest of the cave creatures, lava whales (kehtuhkentem ohbensuhg) grow up to 50 yards long from nose to tail. They live in family pods of half a dozen or so, and are found in rivers or lakes of molten lava or boiling mud. Their appearance is usually that of a muddy "island" in a sea of boiling liquid, since the whole body usually is not visible. Lava whales have legs, something like an otter or seal, so be warned — it is unwise to irritate a lava whale, as it *will* give chase onto dry land!

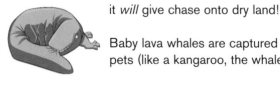

Baby lava whales are captured and kept as pets (like a kangaroo, the whales' young are

Parrot Lizards
Popular as pets, parrot lizards are colorful and friendly.
They can be raised as pets or as food (like rabbits),
and flocks of the things fly wild around Atlantis.
Many varieties of the parrot lizard can be viewed in
the Atlantis Aviary.

tiny compared to the adults) in vats of boiling
mud or molten metal (they have long been popular pets with blacksmiths). Fierce and loyal
protectors of their adopted "families," when the
whales get too big to take care of, they are
returned to the caves.

Special expeditions (Lava Whale Hunts)
are arranged to view the migration of these
majestic creatures seasonally.

Atlantean
Wildflowers
Kehn-Noth, who owns a prominent Atlantean
floral business, leads this seasonal tour. Not
only will participants learn the names and char-
acteristics of many varieties of native flowers,
Kehn-Noth will also discuss the dangers of
some, and the healing, curative, and restorative
powers of others.

Agriculture
in Atlantis
Although the era of the great Plain of Atlantis
is past, this tour combines walking, watercraft,
and hover-vehicle transportation to tell the story
of the farming and cultivation of Atlantean land
and tour the neglected and abandoned sites of
this once-thriving agrarian industry.

The Falls
of Atlantis
After the Cataclysm, Atlantis became a land of
ubiquitous waterfalls. This intimate expedition
combines walking, watercraft, and hover-vehicle
transportation to tour some of the most distinctive and famous of the Atlantis falls, including
the picturesque, the historic, and the terrifying!
Luncheon is taken in the abandoned mill, which
once used a waterfall for industry.

Atlantean Vocabulary

Being a Concise Lexicon of Basic Phrases, Questions, and
Greetings in the Native Tongue

Essential words

Hello	SOO-puhk
Greetings (more formal)	deh-GIHM
Hi!	toakh
Good-bye	GAH-moak
Yes	teeg
No	kwahm
Please [to one]	BEH-ket
[to a group]	BEH-ket-yoakh
Thank you [to one]	PAH-geh-sheh-nen
[to a group]	PAH-geh-sheh-nekh
Thanks [to one]	PAH-gen
[to a group]	PAH-gekh
My name is…	AH-nik KAH-gihn … EH seh-toat
I don't understand.	(kahg) kwahm DOH-yih-neh-kik

Alphabet

a	⊙	n		
b		o		
c		p		
ch		q		
d		r		
e		s		
f		sh		
g		t		
h		th		
i		u		
j		v		
k		w		
l		x		
m		y		
		z		

Numbers

1	dihn	·
2	doot	:
3	say	⁝
4	kut	·|
5	shah		
6	luk	|·
7	tohs	|:
8	yah	|⁝
9	niht	·†
10	EH-khep	†

Useful phrases

Do you speak English?
(moakh) DEEG-tem EHN-luh-nuhg BAH-sheh-beh-nen doo

I don't speak Atlantean.
(kahg) DEEG-tem AHD-luhn-tih-suhg kwahm BAH-sheh-beh-kik

I only speak a little Atlantean.
(kahg) DEEG-tem AHD-luhn-tih-suhg TEE-pihm-mil ser
BAH-sheh-beh-kik

What is this called in Atlantean?
DEE-gesh AHD-luhn-tih-suhg, mekh LEH-guhp EE-muhg neb
EH-seh-toat duhp

Where is the toilet, please?
BEH-ket, luht PEH-wuhd TEE-ku-deh-toat duhp

How much is that?
lohg eem deb MOH-kheh-deh-toat dap

What is your name?
mekh AH-nik MOH-khin EH-seh-toat duhp

Welcome to the city of Atlantis.
WEEL-tem AHD-luhn-tih-suhg net GAH-wih-dihn NAH-geb-yoakh

What time is it?
lohg DAH-rim EH-seh-toat duhp

How do I get to…	lood … kweh-TIH-pek-kihk duhp
a tourist office	NEH-set-tem WEH-geh-noh-suhg
the king's chamber	KEH-loab-tem MAH-kij-tuhg
the marketplace	WEH-ser-tem
the swim chamber	KEH-loab-tem NAH-weh-noh-suhg
Lava Lake	TOH-nen-tem OH-beh-suhg

Where can I rent a…?	luht … LEH-pen BOH-geh-kihk duhp
Ketak	KEH-tuhk-tem
Martag	muhr-TUHG-tem
Aktirak	uhk-TEE-ruhk-tem

Where is the best place from which to view the Lava Whales?
KEH-tuh-ken-tem OH-beh-suhg SAH-poh-kheh-kihk yohs luht nahf
BAH-dehg-bay TEE-ku-deh-toat duhp

Welcome Home

Being a Familiarization with Regulations Regarding
Luggage, Immigration, and Customs

It has been our pleasure to have hosted this remarkable and unforgettable journey. As your visit draws to a close, here are a few instructions and reminders for your departure:

Luggage Luggage tags are provided to assist you in locating your luggage at your destination terminal. Please write your name and home address on these tags. Remove any old train and ship tags and the yellow Whitmore Industries arrival tags. Attach the new tags to your luggage and give the luggage to your final night host or innkeeper by midnight of the evening prior to departure. Any luggage not so delivered must be hand-carried by visitor to the central departure point.

Luggage for our visitors west of the Mississippi may be retrieved from the "Whitmore" pen in the Baggage Claim area at Union Station in Carlsbad, New Mexico.

Luggage for our visitors east of the Mississippi may be retrieved from the Whitmore Industries Field Office in Cave City, Kentucky.

Immigration Atlantean Immigration requires all visitors, including children, to present themselves personally for inspection upon arrival at our point of exit from Atlantis. This includes Canadians and Alien resident cardholders. At this time, bring a completed Customs Declaration Form and your Passport receipts.

For our visitors west of the Mississippi, this agent will be disguised as a U.S. Guano Inspector in Carlsbad, New Mexico. For our visitors east of the Mississippi, this agent will be presented as a Mammoth Caves Official Guide in Cave City, Kentucky.

Settling Your Atlantean Account All transactions within Atlantis should be settled upon your departure. Any outstanding or disputed payments will be billed by mail directly to the visitor by Whitmore Industries (the Invoice will reference the Whitmore Office of Corporate and Dignitary Courtesy).

Customs Allowance In accordance with Atlantean Customs regulations, please be aware of the following: It is required that one visitor per family complete a Customs Declaration Form. The details on the front must be completed fully and you must sign and date the form. Customs Declaration Forms are also available in German, Japanese, French, Spanish, Portuguese, Italian and Choctaw.

You must declare all articles acquired in transit and in your possession at the time of your return. This includes gifts presented to you en route, repairs and alterations made on articles taken abroad and any article included for use or sale in business. Please be prepared to surrender all crystals, herbal remedies, and squid.

U.S. Residents Total duty free allowance per person is $500. Your purchases from all Inner World destinations may be combined to make up the $500 limit.

Total Liquor Allowance One liter of Atlantean wine is the base exemption. All Atlantean wines, port, rum, and specialty liquors must be relabeled with the Whitmore Vineyards imprint prior to departing on the old Atlantis road. NOTE: It is **unlawful** to remove Atlantean Ales from Atlantis.

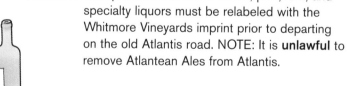

We wish you a safe journey home and look forward to seeing you on another Subterranean Tour in the future. But for now, *pahgehshehnehk, gahmoak ahdluhntihsuhg* — thank you, and farewell to Atlantis!

— P.B.W.

Whitmore Industries

𐌊𐌔𐌗𐌗𐌓𐌔𐌖𐌗 𐌗𐌔 𐌗𐌖𐌗𐌗𐌖𐌔𐌗𐌗𐌗

Welcome to Atlantis

CUSTOMS DECLARATION

**EACH TRAVELER OR RESPONSIBLE FAMILY MEMBER
MUST PROVIDE THE FOLLOWING INFORMATION (ONLY
ONE DECLARATION PER FAMILY IS REQUIRED):**

1. Full Name:

2. Nationality:

3. Country of Residence:

4. Date of Birth (DD-MM-YYYY):

5. Passport Number:

6. Number of Family Members Traveling Together:

7. Address in Atlantis:

TRAVELERS ENTERING ATLANTIS ARE REQUIRED TO DECLARE all perishable goods in their possession. Travelers are responsible for opening their baggage for examination by a Whitmore representative and for repacking their goods after examination. If you have any questions about what must be declared please check with a Whitmore representative.

8. Please check in the appropriate box after reading the notice above.

GOODS TO DECLARE
Proceed to customs examination.

NOTHING TO DECLARE
Please proceed

9. I have read the policy above and certify that this declaration is true.

Signature: _____ *Date:* _____